Henry Wace

The Sacrifice of Christ

Its vital reality and efficacy

Henry Wace

The Sacrifice of Christ
Its vital reality and efficacy

ISBN/EAN: 9783337237165

Printed in Europe, USA, Canada, Australia, Japan

Cover: Foto ©Lupo / pixelio.de

More available books at **www.hansebooks.com**

THE SACRIFICE
OF CHRIST

ITS VITAL REALITY AND EFFICACY

BY

HENRY WACE, D.D.

Prebendary of St Paul's Cathedral Rector of St Michael's Cornhill
Chaplain in Ordinary to the Queen and Examining
Chaplain to the Archbishop of Canterbury
Formerly Preacher of Lincoln's Inn

NEW YORK
THE MACMILLAN COMPANY
1898

PREFACE

THE following pages, written for Lincoln's Inn Chapel, were prompted by a desire to apprehend, if possible, how the Sacrifice of our Saviour, and its atoning efficacy, arose naturally from the circumstances of his life and ministry, and from his relation to the Jews. Much of the difficulty felt on the subject has probably arisen from an impression that the Atonement involved some arbitrary or artificial arrangement, amounting almost to a legal fiction; and thoughtful persons have been perplexed, or even repelled, by the introduction of conceptions of this nature into the profound moral realities of the relations between

God and man. All the rest of our
Saviour's life and work, however beyond our comprehension, is yet felt to
be instinct with a moral and spiritual
life, with which we can enter into real
sympathy; and it would be painful to
regard the most momentous of all His
actions, His Passion and Death, as
less real, and—in the highest sense—
natural. It is hoped that the thoughts
suggested in the following Addresses
will help to remove such difficulties,
and to afford some reverent guidance
into the meaning of Christ's sufferings.
The mystery of His Sacrifice must,
indeed, ever remain in many respects
beyond the apprehension of the human
mind and heart ; but so far as our Lord
Himself has revealed its nature, it is our
duty, as well as our privilege, to follow
His guidance, and that of His Apostles,
in endeavouring to appreciate it. That

guidance has been afforded in some cardinal points which, profound as they are, are still of the most human and most touching character; and there is no truth of our Faith which, when interpreted by the simple language of our Lord and His Disciples, will be found to touch our hearts more closely than that of His Atonement.

The Sacrifice of Christ

THE HISTORY OF THE SACRIFICE

JOHN x. 17.—'Therefore doth my Father love me, because I lay down my life, that I might take it again. No man taketh it from me, but I lay it down of myself. I have power to lay it down, and I have power to take it again. This commandment have I received of my Father.'

THESE words are the key to the history and the preciousness of our Lord's sacrifice ; and in proportion to our appreciation of the light they throw upon the awful scenes in which that sacrifice was consummated will be our apprehension of the Saviour's work for us, and of our obligation to Him. They bring distinctly before us the cardinal fact, that throughout all those scenes of violence and

The Passion was a deliberate action.

A

cruelty of which He was the victim, our Lord was Himself not merely the chief sufferer, but the chief actor. We speak of His Passion, and rightly; but it was a passion in a very different sense from that in which the word could be applied to any mere human being. The Passion of our Lord was a deliberate action, undertaken, and even chosen, by Himself. For the purpose of appreciating this aspect of the Saviour's sufferings, it is desirable we should keep clearly in mind the actual and historical course of the great tragedy which was then enacted. It was a real tragedy, produced by the real and living action of human passions and crimes, and we must remember the various motives at work if we would enter into its meaning.

The last Passover. We have to recollect, then, that our Lord had come up to Jerusalem, at the time of the Passover, with the deliberate intention of asserting His Royal and Messianic authority, and consequently of challenging and superseding the erroneous teaching, and misused authority, of the Scribes and Pharisees, and other rulers of the people. For some two or three years, sometimes in Jerusalem, but mainly in Galilee, He had been establishing His influence and authority as the one Person for whose advent the Jews looked, and some of His immediate disciples had at length been led to recognise Him as the Messiah. He had in consequence obtained a very large following, particularly among the people of Galilee; but His teaching had provoked much opposition from the representatives of the ruling class. For this reason He had carefully avoided, from time to time, any direct encounter with them. But the time came when, in the fulfilment of His mission, it was necessary for Him to confront them, to recall them to the true knowledge and obedience of His Father in heaven, and to require their allegiance to Himself.

With this purpose, He solemnly enters Jerusalem at the time when it was filled by people from all parts of the country; and He deliberately makes His entry in such a way as to assert His royal claims. He entered riding upon an ass, ' that it

The entry into Jerusalem

might be fulfilled which was spoken by
the prophet, saying, Tell ye the daughter
of Sion, Behold thy King cometh unto
thee, meek, and sitting upon an ass.'
The significance of this entry was recognized. ' The multitudes that went before,
and that followed, cried, saying, Hosanna
to the Son of David ; Blessed is He that
cometh in the name of the Lord.' So
that when they were come to Jerusalem
' all the city was moved, saying, Who
is this ? ' The next day He went into
the Temple, and proceeded to assert
His authority in the most unmistakable
manner, by driving out from it the
traders, by whom it was profaned, and
quoting against them the words, ' My
house shall be called the house of
prayer, but ye have made it a den of
thieves.' He further manifested His
miraculous and Divine authority by
working miracles. ' The blind and the
lame came to Him in the Temple, and
He healed them.'

The mutual challenge. The consequence was that, the next
day, He was formally challenged by the
chief priests and the elders to state by

what authority He assumed these offices
and powers. It was in itself not an unnatural nor an illegitimate question. A
person who entered the Temple in royal
state, and proceeded to claim the right
of purging it of abuses, in the face of
its constituted governors, ought to be
able to state the authority by which
he acted. But, in this case, the chief
priests might have known, and in fact
did know, by what authority our Lord
acted ; and He accordingly at once
threw back the responsibility on them
by His counter question : ' The baptism
of John, whence was it ? From heaven,
or of men ? ' John had been His
authoritative forerunner, and it had
been his mission to prepare the hearts
of the people for Him. Those who
believed John were prepared, by John's
preaching and discipline, to believe our
Lord Himself; but unless men accepted
the authority of John, they were not
in a moral condition for accepting our
Lord's authority. The chief priests
refused to answer. They knew that
if they acknowledged John's Divine

mission, they must acknowledge our Lord's; and this they were resolved not to do. But they feared the people, who held John to be a prophet; and so they answered, 'We cannot tell.'

Two claims in conflict. From that moment two conflicting claims were in direct opposition. Our Lord had claimed a Divine mission and authority over the very Temple itself, and consequently over the rulers of the Temple; and they felt that His claims were subversive of their own teaching, and of their position. They therefore set themselves in deadly antagonism to Him; and He, on His part, from that time abandoned all reserve, and proceeded to attack and denounce them with a severity, a directness, and an intensity unparalleled. In parable after parable, and denunciation after denunciation, He attacks their hypocrisy, their hardness of heart, their blindness to the deepest moral and spiritual truths, their faithlessness to the great trust committed to them, and their rebellion against their God. He discharges this terrible office with indignation, but at the same time with pity—breaking down, as it were, after His fiercest denunciation, into the infinitely pathetic lament: 'O Jerusalem, Jerusalem, thou that killest the prophets, and stonest them which are sent unto thee, how often would I have gathered thy children together, even as a hen gathereth her chickens under her wings, and ye would not!' He warns them of the terrible destruction which must come upon them if they persisted in their obstinacy, and He foresees the bitter agony which His action must bring upon Himself. But He does not hesitate or withdraw for an instant. From the moment when His authority had been challenged, the record of the Gospels describes a terrible series of assaults on the whole position of the chief priests and elders. We see one onset following another, on their wavering, recoiling, breaking and retreating forces, until the struggle has been brought to a critical issue, and the question must be decided, whether He or they shall be recognized as representing the authority of God, and of religious and moral truth.

The issue at stake. Now, if we realize that our Lord was thus engaged in a final endeavour to assert His royal and Divine authority over the rulers and people of the chosen race—that He was doing this in His Father's name, and for the purpose of the due establishment of that Father's authority, we shall see what a tremendous issue was raised when the rulers finally rejected Him. Two authorities and two claims are in direct conflict : the claim and the authority of God Himself, represented by His own Son, and the perverted claims and authority of the chief priests and scribes. If we could for a moment forget what the actual conduct of our Lord was, and could look at the crisis from a human point of view, what could be expected but such a manifestation of divine wrath and justice, as would overwhelm the opponents of God and His Christ ? The contest between God and man is brought in these great scenes to a direct issue—an issue more direct than has ever been presented before or since. God incarnate, exhibiting the very truth, justice, goodness, mercy, love, and power of the divine nature, stands before His chosen people, before their rulers and teachers, and demands their allegiance ; and they deny His authority, and take counsel to put Him to death. What is before us, is not simply that a perfectly good man is being spurned, and his witness rejected. It is not only that a prophet is endeavouring to arouse the hearts of the people to a truer apprehension of righteousness, and to confession of sin. Our Lord is much more than a prophet; He is the Son of God Himself, making the most direct and intense appeal which God could make to His creatures, adjuring them, in human form, by exhortation, by argument, by parable, by denunciation, by miracle, by mercies, and even by tears, to open their hearts to Him, and acknowledge Him as their true Lord and Master. But they are impervious to all His efforts, and repay Him with insult, hatred, and deadly malice. What is to be the result?

How is the
issue to be
decided?

It is to be remembered that there appears to be no weapon left in the Divine armoury, no means available which have not been tried. Through nearly two thousand years, since the call of their forefather Abraham, has God been training this people as His chosen race, that they might reverence and obey His Son when they saw Him. Law, and prophecy, and national judgments, a last appeal from the greatest of the prophets, and finally, a Divine ministry of infinite mercy and grace— all have been tried. But all have failed; and God Himself, in the person of His own Son in human form, is, so to say, face to face with a determined rebellion, and a direct rejection of Himself, at the hands of His own subjects. What remains, so far as man's judgment could go, but an assertion, by Divine power, of the Divine right? What remains but that 'the King should speak unto them in His wrath, and vex them in His sore displeasure,' that He should

'break them with a rod of iron, and
dash them in pieces like a potter's
vessel?' Our Lord had Himself
described, in one of His parables of
warning, what is the natural course for
the vindication of rightful authority in
such circumstances. In the parable of
the householder, his servants were one
after another rejected, until he sent
unto them his son, 'saying, They will
reverence my son.' But 'they caught
him, and cast him out of the vineyard,
and slew him. When the lord therefore of the vineyard cometh,' our Lord
had asked them, 'what will he do unto
those husbandmen?' And they had
been forced to answer, 'He will miser-
ably destroy those wicked men, and will
let out his vineyard to other husbandmen, which shall render him the fruits
in their seasons.'

In a word, when authority challenges
authority, and neither will give way, The arbitrament of
force.
the only arbitrament remaining is that
of force. One or other must be crushed.
Which, then, is to be crushed in this
case? The question is the most solemn

and momentous that can be conceived.
Is God to be defeated? Are His rebellious children to overcome Him, to
cast out His Son, and to triumph over
His will—that is, over supreme wisdom,
supreme goodness, and supreme power?
It seems inconceivable. Yet that, so
far as concerned the immediate conflict
between the Jewish rulers and our Lord,
is the issue involved. They were determined to kill Him if they had the power.
The only alternative, to human eyes,
was that He should destroy them, and
establish His dominion, and vindicate His
Father's authority, by a supreme and
victorious display of Divine vengeance
and righteousness. It is evident from
the narrative that they recognized that
the conflict was of this deadly character ;
they feared that He might appeal to
popular force, and overthrow them by
that means ; as is said again and again,
' They feared the people.' They did
not believe, they would not recognize,
that He had other powers at His dis-
posal. But they were sensible that they
had challenged Him to the death, and

that one or other of the two foes must
be overwhelmed by force.

But at this point appears, under the Our Lord's resolve.
light afforded us by our knowledge of
our Lord's nature, the gracious marvel
of His mercy. He knew, better than
they did, that the question was one
of death for Himself or for them. He
knew, moreover, as they did not, that
He could in one moment overwhelm
them. It rested with him, with His
free choice, to utter the word which
would have brought upon those rebels
and murderers instant and final destruction. As the son of God, to whom
the Father had committed all judgment,
He had but to utter one prayer to His
Father, and all the thunders and light-
nings of the Divine wrath were at His
command, to overpower the resistance
which was offered to Him. ' Thinkest
thou,' He said to one of His disciples
at the critical moment—'thinkest thou
that I cannot now pray to my father,
and He shall presently give me more
than twelve legions of angels ? ' Every
consideration, moreover, of Divine Jus-

tice, of His own claims and His Father's, would have justified, and seemed to require, such a course. What a crisis! Conceive those heavenly hosts, who, as St Peter says, watch these mysterious scenes, desiring to look unto them, but not knowing the Divine counsels—conceive them beholding God incarnate on the point of being put to death by His enemies—and what would be their expectation? Can He hesitate to crush them? Mysterious resolve! He deliberately and quietly takes the other alternative, and allows them to crush Him. As one or other of the antagonists must die, He will die.

His choice of self-sacrifice.   It is only in the light of this amazing resolve that we read the story of the Passion aright. This is not the passion of a martyr, whose only choice is between denying the truth and suffering for the truth's sake. Our Lord has the power of instantly vindicating the truth by crushing His adversaries. It is not merely that He has the power of delivering Himself—that is not the point in the contest. The question is one of sub-

mission to the King of truth; and He has
the power of enforcing that submission
by showing His supremacy over His
enemies, and executing a just vengeance
on those who denied the truth. But He
deliberately chose to die Himself, and
to submit to all the misery which ac-
companied that death, rather than vindicate His authority by the punishment
and destruction of His adversaries. As
was observed at the outset, this is
much more than a passion. At every
moment throughout that Passion the
Saviour is deliberately restraining Himself, by an act of will, from asserting the
power, the Divine and righteous power,
by which, in an instant, He might have
not only saved, but asserted Himself.
It rested with Him, at every moment
through that long torture and agony, to
say whether He or His opponents should
suffer; and He chooses to suffer Himself. That fierce culmination of human
evil, that deadly conflict between right
and wrong, between God and His adver-
sary, must have a victim; that is in the
very nature of the case; and although,

by all the laws of justice, the victim should be the offender, our Lord submits, almost in silence, to be the victim Himself.

The love and mercy of our Lord. Various consequences, to be considered in subsequent discourses, follow from this aspect of our Saviour's Passion. Our belief in the reality of this aspect of it rests, it may be well at once to observe, partly on our Lord's own declaration in the text, quoted from St John, and finally on the evidence afforded by His resurrection. The fact that He rose again, according to His own promise, gives a final and abundant confirmation of His assurance, that it was of His own free will that He laid down His life. No man took that life from Him, but He laid it down of Himself. He had power to lay it down, as He had power to take it again. But it may be enough, for the present, to ask whether these simple historical considerations do not of themselves afford us a living and vivid apprehension of our Lord's love and mercy, which ought to maintain in our souls the deepest and most vital feeling of gratitude and devotion. We have seen the manner in which, in the moment of final decision, He dealt with the sins of men while He was upon earth. He had to decide in one supreme moment, and to maintain the decision through a long agony, whether men should die for their sins, or whether He should die instead; and He then chose to die Himself, in order, so to say, that they might have a final respite. It is not merely, therefore, in a doctrinal sense, but with a living apprehension of what He had himself witnessed, that St Peter says: 'He bare our sins in His own body on the tree.' To that death, voluntarily accepted, we owe it that we live in a time of grace, and that the Divine long-suffering still bears with the revolt of the human heart —of our own hearts and lives—against the Divine righteousness. Our Lord is still submitting, as He did then, to the neglect of men, to their unbelief, to their rebellion. He is still making a last and final appeal to all mankind, as He did to those who crucified Him, by dying in the stead of His enemies, and bearing that final witness to the truth and love they are rejecting. But He cannot die again. The time must come, when the conflict between Divine righteousness and human sin will be brought to a decision, and when those who have not submitted by faith to the Saviour's authority, or rather to the Saviour's love, must be left to suffer the Divine justice. But what can surpass the intensity of the obligation under which our Saviour's death brought His enemies, and under which He has brought every human soul, by thus choosing to suffer rather than that they should die, and winning for them, by this offering of Himself, a final opportunity of becoming reconciled to Himself and to His Father? In a word, what a living grace, what a profound personal appeal, does not this first and simplest aspect of the Saviour's death give to the words of His Apostle, telling us that ' He Himself bare our sins in His own body on the tree, that we, being dead to sins, should live unto righteousness ; by whose stripes we were healed.'

THE EFFICACY OF THE SACRIFICE

2 COR. v. 19-21.—'God was in Christ, reconciling the world unto Himself, not imputing their trespasses unto them ; and hath committed unto us the word of reconciliation. Now then we are ambassadors for Christ, as though God did beseech you by us : we pray you in Christ's stead, that ye be reconciled to God. For He hath made Him to be sin for us, who knew no sin, that we might be made the righteousness of God in Him.'

IN the previous discourse we considered the actual history of our Lord's suffering, as exhibiting the facts which constitute the atonement He offered in order to reconcile His Father to us, and to be a sacrifice for the sins of the world ; and the main point which demanded our attention, as stated by Himself and by His Apostles, was that He voluntarily took upon Himself consequences which,

The voluntary action of our Lord in His sacrifice.

in the nature of the case, would have
fallen upon those by whom He was crucified. His resurrection is the final proof
of His saying that He had power to lay
down His life, as He had power to take
it again—that no man took it from Him,
but that He laid it down of Himself—that
He had power to lay it down, and power
to take it again. This is the first, if not
the most important, point, in which the
resurrection illuminates the whole character of our Lord's work on earth.
Had He disappeared after death, there
would have been no definite evidence
that His death was more than that of
a perfectly good man—a death, therefore, which He could not have avoided,
and which had no more merit than that
of a perfectly true and faithful martyr.
But His resurrection proves that, not-
withstanding all the force and violence
of which He was the victim, He possessed
powers which, as they raised Him from
the grave, could have saved Him from
it ; and that in the endurance of His
suffering and His death He was throughout the chief actor, as abstaining from

the use of means by which He could,
at any moment, have saved Himself.

But the reason, for which He thus The reason for this voluntary Passion.
abstained from calling on His Father
for those legions of Angels, whom His
prayer might have brought to His side,
was that the only alternative to suffering
Himself was to inflict suffering and
destruction on His enemies. He and
the rulers of the Jewish people .were
at war; His authority, or rather His
Father's, and theirs were in deadly
conflict; and they, on their part, had
resolved that they would terminate
the conflict by the only possible issue,
so far as they could see, of putting
Him to death. But rather than vindicate His Father's authority, and deliver
Himself, at the cost of the destruction
and misery of His people, He consented
patiently to be put to death Himself;
and, at that cost, He, so to say, respited
the assertion of the Divine righteousness
in conflict with human sin, and established the deepest and most touching of
all conceivable claims to the acceptance
of His message, and submission to His

Father's authority. He had appealed
to men's sense of righteousness and
truth in vain ; He would now appeal to
their capacity for gratitude and love ;
and before the final judgment by which
the righteousness of God must, at last,
be vindicated and established, He would
hang upon the cross before the whole
world, in attestation that He could
not waver in the assertion of the Divine
Will, but that He would Himself
suffer the utmost misery, and the in-
tensest agonies of death, rather than
resort to the only mode of enforcing
Divine justice which could be afforded
by the ordinary action of the moral law.

The neces-
sity of an
adequate
vindication
of the moral
law.

Now it would seem not difficult to
perceive that this voluntary endurance
of the consequences of human sin on
our Saviour's part answered, at all events,
the chief ends of a punitive infliction of
Divine justice. There is some danger,
no doubt, in pursuing the *à priori* argu-
ments, by which divines, some of them
of the highest authority, have endea-
voured to show the necessity of the infliction of a specific equivalent for the

offence offered to Divine justice by the sin of man. Apart from the consideration that any such exact knowledge of the necessities of Divine justice may well be deemed beyond our faculties, it would seem difficult to argue, even from our own apprehensions of justice, to the necessity of any such equivalence between the offence and the penalty. Certainly the world is not governed, nor are human relations maintained, on the principle of an eye for an eye and a tooth for a tooth; and it would be contrary to one of the most characteristic principles of our Lord's teaching to doubt that the Divine action corresponds with the most generous instincts which He has implanted in our nature. But, at the same time, if we abstain from these rigid and abstract definitions, we cannot fail to recognize the absolute necessity of some adequate vindication of Divine justice—in common language, of an example being made. A law which has no sanction, in the technical sense of that expression—in other words, a law which can be broken without an adequate penalty, is no law at all; and it is inconceivable that God's moral law can be violated without entailing consequences of the most terrible kind. The mere violation of one of His physical laws may entail, whether men intend the violation or not, the most widespread and lasting misery; and can it reasonably be supposed that the most flagrant and wilful violation of the highest of all laws—those of truth and righteousness — should entail no such results? In point of fact, the very education of mankind is conducted by means of the strict enforcement of the consequences of breaking established laws. Natural laws assert themselves for the most part, and men have to obey them, because in their every-day life they are punished if they do not. The education of the moral nature of man is, primarily, of the same character. Punishments and rewards are merely the moral form in which laws are enforced which depend on the action of free will. When, then, human nature, in the persons of the Jews, had risen in determined revolt against the incarnation of all truth and righteousness, and, in the person of the heathen Governor, had exhibited a complete indifference to such truth, the very foundations of the moral constitution of the world would have been destroyed, had not some momentous example been given of the ruinous consequences which such rebellion and such indifference must entail.

The natural mode in which such an ex-ample would have been made was by the punishment of the offenders themselves ; and when they persisted in the offence, in spite of the overpowering appeal made to them by our Lord's self-sacrifice, the judgment did fall upon them, in the destruction of their city and their nation. But when our Lord, in the first instance, chose to suffer in their place, when He said in effect, according to the unconscious prophecy of the High Priest, 'It is expedient that one man should die for the people, and that the whole nation perish not,' and when He endured, in the face of the world, those sufferings of the cross, He did exhibit, for the horror and awe of the moral

This vindication afforded by our Lord's voluntary suffering.

universe, how fearful are the consequences of a defiance of Divine justice,
and how tremendous are the sanctions
by which the Divine Will is maintained.
The suffering, which sin and evil entail,
was, in fact, enforced, and enforced in
such a manner as to impress upon the
human heart and conscience the mon-
strosity and shame of sin, even more intensely than would have been practicable
by the mere infliction of punishment on
those who deserved it.   We all know, in
daily life, that the wrong of an evil
action is constantly brought home to
men's hearts far more keenly by the
sight of the suffering which it entails on
some innocent person, than by any consequences which the offending person
himself may endure. That it should
have been necessary, that it should have
been a natural and inevitable consequence of the conduct of the Jewish
rulers and of Pilate, that Christ should
suffer as He did, if the wrath of God
was not to be inflicted on His persecutors—this must constitute, to all
time, the most intense and penetrating

evidence that could be afforded of the abominable character of human evil, and of the wrath which it necessarily evokes from the righteous nature of God. But the evidence has been afforded ; the example has been made ; and without presuming to estimate the exact nature of the requirements of Divine righteousness, we may surely feel that the demands of justice, so far as the human conscience can apprehend them, are satisfied, if God graciously condescends to say that that awful example is enough to vindicate His moral law, once and for all ; and that, except so far as may be necessary for the education of men themselves, He has no longer any occasion to exact any further penalty. Chastisement, in the sense of reformatory discipline, is inherent in the present constitution of things. But punishment, for the sole purpose of vindicating God's justice, is no longer required. The Saviour has chosen to suffer enough for that purpose, and the punitive claims of the moral law are so far satisfied.

This suffering endured by God Himself in human form.

But the nature of our Saviour's action in this respect is but imperfectly apprehended, unless we consider, more particularly, Who it was who thus suffered, the Just for the unjust. The text opens to us the profoundest and most moving feature of this great sacrifice. To refer again, in passing, to the speculations of divines of all ages on this point — much *à priori* argument has been adduced, to prove that no mere human being could ever have offered an adequate satisfaction to the Divine justice; and we may at least be sure, from the universal experience of humanity, that no human being, born after the flesh, could ever have represented the claims of Divine righteousness to men, or could have suffered with that power to lay down His life or to take it again, which constituted so essential an element in our Saviour's work, as we have been considering it. But it is safer for us to contemplate what were the actual facts of the case, rather than to inquire what it was necessary they should be. In point of fact, the work of our Saviour derives its highest significance from the truth, which constitutes the cardinal point of our faith, that He was really God in human form. It was not merely a perfect man who was suffering for the sins of His fellows, rather than be delivered from it by a Divine inter-position which would have crushed them. It was God Himself, Who had taken that human nature upon Him in order to appeal to His creatures in flesh and blood, and to reconcile them to Himself. We are here, in the few words of St Paul in the text, with all they involve, plunged into the depths of those mysteries of the Trinity and the Incarnation, which even the angels desire to look into. Our Lord reveals Himself as the Son of God, acting in strict obedi-ence to the will of the Father, and having it as His sole object to carry that will into effect. He appears, indeed, as a human being, experiencing all the bitterness and agony of which human nature is capable. But the Divine nature and the Divine will are also acting in His Person, and we have to contemplate the whole of the work on His part, which culminated in His suffering and death, as the direct action of God. God was in Christ.

Apply, then, to this view of the sacred Sufferer the considerations we have been reviewing. God, in the Person of His Son, had come into the world, to make a direct appeal to men's hearts, in flesh and blood. He had sent prophet after prophet, but at length He appeared Himself, and spoke to them face to face, and as man to man, striving, by the exertion of every influence which could appeal to their moral, intellectual and physical nature, to win them to submission to His authority and will. But they rebelled. What could follow, according to all ordinary laws, but that they should take the consequences? When every method of appeal has been exhausted, what remained but punishment? But instead of this, God took the consequences on Himself, and accepted, in human form, the punishment which would naturally have fallen on His rebellious creatures. The mystery of the Trinity, involving the mutual action of

the Divine Persons within the Godhead,
alone makes such a conception possible;
and the long and anxious controversies
of Christian theology are no more than
a natural result of the difficulty, which
the human mind must experience, of
attaining any adequate expression, or apprehension, of such truths. But, though
language must be very carefully used on
such topics, we do not enter into the
full significance of the Atonement, unless
we bear in mind that the suffering involved in it was not merely borne by a
human being, but was inflicted on a
human nature in the most essential
union with the Divine Nature itself.
God could not suffer in His Divine
Nature; but He adopted into Himself
a human nature, in which He could, in
a certain sense, suffer; and it was God
Himself, in Christ, Who was bearing
the consequences of human sin, rather
than inflict those consequences on His
creatures. The Atonement of Christ on
the cross is thus essentially an exhibition of Divine love, not merely, nor so
much, in its original intention, as in its

execution.   Men had directly challenged God to the assertion of His authority against them.   They had hardened their hearts against His truth and righteousness, and rendered themselves liable, in the highest possible degree, to the vindication of His laws and the infliction of His wrath.   But He Himself, rather than resort to these terrible measures of justice, prefers to bear, in the nature He has assumed, the consequences of their sin, and submits to be spurned, and mocked, and crucified, that He may appeal to them by one final and supreme influence, and that He may divert to Himself the consequences they had brought upon themselves.   Could there be a higher exhibition of love?   'Herein,' says the Apostle, 'is love, not that we loved God, but that He loved us, and sent His Son to be the propitiation for our sins.'

The sacrifice vicarious as endured by God Himself instead of men.

It is surely perplexing, from this point of view, to understand where the difficulty, so often urged, of vicarious sacrifice and punishment can so much as arise.   If the Holy Person Who bore our sins on the tree had been selected, by Divine choice and power, from among God's creatures, as a sort of substitute for the rest of mankind, it is easy to see how such difficulties would present themselves. But when the Person Who suffers for us is our own Judge, our own Creator, Who, of His own supremely free will, chooses to take upon Himself the consequences which His laws would otherwise have entailed upon His creatures, what room is there for anything but adoring gratitude at such a voluntary act of supreme self-sacrifice on our behalf? The fact before us is, simply, that the last effort of Divine love, in endeavouring to win the human heart to Himself, is to take upon Himself, in a peculiarly bitter experience, the consequences men had brought upon themselves. God cannot abolish that moral constitution of things which He has established, and unless men will submit to it in the end, it must take effect upon them in all its terrible judgment. But He has taken upon Himself the consequences of this violation of His law in

C

their most bitter form, in order that no
necessities of mere punitive justice, at
all events, shall stand in the way of His
complete forgiveness of His creatures,
and that He may prove to them that
the laws, from which they shrink, and
which they strive to evade, are enforced
by Him in the deepest love, and in the
most perfect sympathy with themselves.
He is in Christ reconciling the world unto
Himself, not imputing their trespasses
unto them—not holding them, as yet,
to the responsibility of their sin, even
though it be so great as to proceed to
the murder of His Son.

The highest
exhibition of
His love.
Such, according to the statements of
our Lord and of His Apostles, seems to be
the actual explanation of the momentous
circumstances of our Lord's sufferings
and death.   Those events are certainly
the most momentous in the history of
mankind, and it is trifling with the
deepest experiences of human nature not
to endeavour to realize and apprehend
them.   According to the Apostles, they
are nothing less than a revelation of the
love of God in bearing the consequences

of our sins Himself, in order that, if possible, we may be spared those consequences. They are intended to bring home to us, in the most affecting form, the loving will of God that we should accept His truth and submit to His righteousness; and He not merely requires us to do this, or exhorts us to it, but suffers with us and for us, in the human nature He has assumed, in order that He may save us by the manifold influences of that suffering. Contemplate God in Christ, thus reconciling the world to Himself, and how can we fail to respond to the appeal which follows?—'We pray you in Christ's stead, be ye reconciled to God.' He Himself 'bare our sins in His own body on the tree, that we, being dead to sins, should live unto righteousness.'

I I I

PERSONAL EFFECT OF THE SACRIFICE

1 John ii. 1, 2.—'My little children these things write I unto you, that ye sin not. And if, any man sin, we have an Advocate with the Father, Jesus Christ the righteous : and He is the propitiation for our sins : and not for ours only, but also for the sins of the whole world.'

The personal character of our Lord's sacrifice. THE considerations which have been already reviewed with respect to the Sacrifice offered by our Lord · have served, it may be hoped, to illustrate the living and personal character which it bears. It has been a danger in theological thought on this subject, from even the earliest times, to lay such stress on some of the images, by which that Atonement is illustrated in the Scriptures, as to present it in the light

of a kind of formal and material transaction ; as though it consisted, for
example, in the payment of a ransom or
the discharge of a debt. Even in the
early Church, this conception took the
strange form of a ransom being paid to
the evil one ; and the nobler apprehension of the mystery which is due to
St Anselm, the great Archbishop of
Canterbury, has been observed to be
too much pervaded by feudal conceptions of the satisfaction by which
offences against superiors, or against an
external law, could be expiated. There
are, no doubt, points of analogy between our Saviour's atonement and such
human relations ; but there is a serious
danger in allowing ourselves to be guided
by artificial human institutions in considering the relations between ourselves
and God. The natural and permanent
relations of human life—those of Father-
hood, Sonship, Brotherhood, Government,
and Justice—are real reflections of the
relations between God and man ; and
we are constantly taught by our Lord,
in His parables, to judge by them of our

duty to God and of His will towards us. But just as the Mosaic Law itself, with its Divinely ordered regulations, fell away at once before the revelation of the eternal laws of religion and morality in Christ, so must any artificial rule of action, any law due to special forms of human society and experience, be put aside, when considering the deepest and most essential elements of God's relation to us.

The natural course of the history.

Accordingly, we have seen that the course of events which brought about our Saviour's sacrifice was due to no arbitrary arrangement, but was the result of the natural action, and counteraction, of human sin and Divine righteousness and goodness. The revolt of men against God, exhibited in the rejection of our Lord by the Jewish people, involved of necessity a tremendous convulsion. It was the most deadly conflict which could possibly arise in the moral order of the world ; and the Divine justice must, in some way, be vindicated. In the ordinary course of Divine government that justice would be vindicated by the punishment and destruction of those who had rebelled against it. Moral laws must assert themselves as much, at least, as all other laws. But at this crisis our Lord, instead of at once bringing punishment upon those who had rejected Him and denied His Father, chose to bear the consequences of that moral revolt Himself; and instead of destroying His enemies, submitted Himself to be put to death. He thus bore witness in His own sacred Person, for all time and eternity, of the bitter consequences which, in the natural order of things, ensue from men's violation of their duty to God and to one another; and at the same time, being God as well as man, He bore witness to men of the infinite love and patience with which God deals with them. He assumed human form in order that, so to say, the whole moral drama of life might work itself out around Him, and that righteousness and sin might wage their terrible conflict in and around His own person; and when that dreadful battle—the real

battle of the world—led to the necessity
of a choice whether He or His enemies
should suffer, He preferred, in the first
instance, to suffer Himself. The eternal
laws God had impressed upon the
moral world worked themselves out, in
our Saviour's life, to this fearful issue.
In the brief, but luminous, narrative of
the Gospels, we behold that great moral
conflict at its full intensity, and we see
to what human nature comes when it
revolts against God. But the Saviour
makes Himself one with this sinning
and rebellious race, and diverts upon
His own head the wrath and vengeance
they were bringing on themselves. By
this means, in the person of His Son,
God appeals to men by the one influence of which the manifestation had
previously been impracticable—by that
of unbounded love and self-sacrifice.
He took a human nature into the most
intimate and essential union with Himself, and chose to suffer in it, in order
to exhibit to men the consequences of
their own evil, to provide an adequate
satisfaction to His own righteousness,

and to win their hearts by such an exhibition of long-suffering and love.

What we see, therefore, is not simply a ransom paid, or a debt discharged. We see the personal, living and mutual action of the Father, the Son, and of human beings. God is actually appealing to the Jews, and striving to bring home His claims to them; they are struggling against these claims, even to the desperate extent of putting to death the Lord Who is His witness to them ; and He, the Lord whom they are thus rejecting, is seen pleading with them to the last, and in patience bearing their insults and their cruelty, refusing to call upon His Father for those spiritual legions which might have delivered Him ; praying, on the contrary, 'Father, forgive them, for they know not what they do'; and, when He had died for them, rising again, and sending His servants to plead with them once more, and to entreat them, by the mercies He had shown to them, to return to Him. It is a tragedy of a similar kind to that which may too often be seen in our daily

The Divine sacrifice and appeal.

life. Someone's misconduct may entail the most cruel consequences to a near relation—to a father, a wife, or a brother ; but the injured person, instead of asserting his own rights, and bringing the just consequences of the wrong-doing upon the offender, will take them as far as possible upon himself, from no other motive than the hope of giving the wrong-doer an opportunity of recovery, and of placing him under the strongest obligation to that recovery, by such an exhibition of self-sacrifice. The wronged relation, the husband, the wife, or the brother, will make on behalf of the offender all the reparation that is practicable. He will endeavour, as we say, to atone for the offence. We can well conceive him pleading with others to have regard to the sacrifice he is himself making for his friend, his wife, or his child, and he will patiently bear the injury he himself suffers, if only he can save another from destruction. It would be a small matter, in such a case, if a friend merely paid a ransom, or discharged a debt, and then went away.

The highest examples of such vicarious suffering consist in the patient love, which is constantly exerted in bearing the consequences of another's sins, for the sake of that other's recovery. This is what was done by our Lord in the case of the Jews. He personally stood between them and the just anger of God, and He appealed to them, on the ground of that sacrifice, to accept and obey Him.

But let us now advance to the further consideration, that the relation of God to men at all times, and His relation to ourselves at this time, is of precisely the same character. We are not, according to the Scriptures, to regard Him as having simply established a moral world, as a kind of moral machine, in which laws operate as they do in physical nature. But He is Himself continually in personal relation with us, just as He was with the Jews of our Lord's day. What we see, therefore, in the life of our Lord, is but a visible manifestation of what is proceeding in the daily life of every soul among us. Under the Christian

The permanent relation of men to God.

dispensation, we are brought within the circle of the Divine life in a more intimate degree than was the case before. The Divine Spirit has been sent into the world, to convince men of sin, of righteousness, and of judgment; and the Christian conscience is the result of that continual communion between the soul of man and its Father in heaven. God's relation to our daily life and daily conduct is, accordingly, one of continuous personal knowledge and personal judgment. The Spirit, Whom our Lord said He would send into the world, was to be a personal agent like Himself, forming personal judgments of our conduct, just as our Lord formed them of the disciples who were with Him, or of the Jews to whom He bore His testimony. In a word, we are in daily and hourly relation with a personal and righteous Lord, whose relations to us, of approbation or disapprobation, of pleasure or displeasure, of love and of wrath, are substantially similar to those which prevail between ourselves. A living God is perpetually forming a moral judgment of our actions, bearing witness to our inmost hearts of what is right and wrong in us, and regarding us in accordance with our moral and religious conduct. We have to do, not simply with an established order, but with a living personality—with a living God.

Is it not strange that any obscurity should ever have been cast upon the momentous import of such a revelation of our position? The question whether we are dealing simply with moral laws, or with a living moral Being, is one which goes to the very roots of human thought and experience. To realize that we are in the presence of a living Person, Who is always judging us, Whose eyes are upon us in the light and in the dark, and from Whom we can never escape—this is a conception of infinite awe, as compared simply with the apprehension that we are subject to certain laws and circumstances. 'As in water face answereth to face, so the heart of man to man,' and above all, the heart of man to a

His personal and continual judgment of us.

perfect man. There, and there alone, in the face of a living personality, human and Divine, do our thoughts and words and actions find their real reflection and their real judgment. But it is involved in this revelation, we must bear in mind, that the Divine nature, with which we are thus in contact, must be perpetually exerting its moral judgment upon us. It is the very nature of God that He should be ever living and ever acting. He is perpetually bringing His righteousness to bear upon our conduct ; and the various attributes of His nature must be in perpetual action towards our own souls. Granted, that in such language, we are speaking by analogy, and to some extent figuratively. The question is whether it be a true analogy, and a substantially just figure. In speaking of the Divine nature we cannot avoid analogies and figures of speech. In its own ˌsubstance, that nature must remain incomprehensible and inexpressible by any finite mind, and it can only be partially revealed to us by the things, and by the persons, it has created. But God must be more revealed by the highest things He has created than by the lowest, and the truest images of the Divine nature and action must be drawn from those personal beings, in whom we recognize the highest visible development of creation. The Divine life and action, in short, is infinitely higher than any description of it in human language; but if it be true to say—as all who speak of it at all will admit—that it works by laws, that it observes an order, that it displays energy ; then it is right and necessary to say, also, that it exerts moral judgments, that it exercises a personal and moral action upon our own individual souls.

If this be so, one conclusion is inevitable—that the moral wrong continually wrought by men, continually wrought by ourselves, must evoke a continuous action of moral displeasure—in other words, of righteous wrath—from the Divine Nature. A moral nature without that quality which, as distinguished from

The wrath of God.

mere passion, we denote as moral re-
sentment, is inconceivable ; and we are
consequently forced to the awful consideration that, in our relations with
God, in our continual disobedience to
His Will, in our violations of right, and
our failure to obey His voice in our
consciences, we are perpetually provok-
ing His anger.   If it be said that God
is love, let it not be supposed that this
is in the slightest degree inconsistent
with the truth that He is a God of just
wrath.   If you mean anything intelligible
by love, you mean a moral quality ; and
you cannot suppose the moral quality
of love to subsist without the moral
quality of righteousness subsisting by
the side of it, with the judgment which
such righteousness involves.

Its action
restrained by
our Lord's
perpetual in-
terposition.
The view of our position which these
considerations should bring before us is,
in short, that we not merely have to
appear hereafter before the judgment-
seat of Christ, but that we are living
momentarily in relation to a just and
Holy Being, whose wrath must be
evoked by the evil doing of men, just

as it was evoked, in the time of our
Lord upon earth, by the evil doing of
the Jewish people. If this be so, what
is it that restrains the Divine Will
from punishing the daily and hourly
offences which we commit? What is
it which prevents the assertion of His
righteous judgment against the terrible
sins by which life is marred all around
us? Where is the influence which
enables Him, consistently with justice
to His own righteousness, with justice
to those claims of right and wrong
which even men desire to see asserted,
to abstain from such a severe enforcement of His laws as would, we must be
well aware, bring misery and disaster
upon us? The answer is to be found in
that aspect of the Atonement which we
have been considering in the history of
our Lord's sacrifice upon earth, and
which the text brings before us. Just
as we are perpetually in personal relation with God, so is our Lord Jesus
Christ in perpetual personal communion
with His Father and with us; and He
is perpetually interposing on our behalf,

with the same love as that with which
He suffered on behalf of His people on
earth, and by virtue of that suffering.

'We have an
advocate
with the
Father.'

'If any man sin,' says the Apostle,
'we have an Advocate with the Father,
Jesus Christ the righteous, and He is
the propitiation for our sins.' The
Apostle does not say merely that, if any
man sin, Jesus Christ has made a propitiation for our sins. That He made
that propitiation, that He offered a
sacrifice, once for all, sufficient for the
vindication of the Divine justice, is,
indeed, elsewhere asserted, and is the
necessary foundation for His action.
But the essential point of the consola-
tion, which the Apostle mentions, is
that by virtue of this propitiation, once
offered, and for ever subsisting in His
own person, our Lord is the perpetual
Advocate of each individual soul with His
Father. He pleads for each one of us,
in our worst sins, as well as in our weaknesses—pleads for us with that sympathy with the weakness of our flesh
which is rendered possible by His
participation of our nature, and with

that claim upon His Father's mercy
which He established by bearing the
consequences of our sins when He was
upon earth. His living presence with
His Father and with us renders His
sacrifice an ever-present, an ever-sub-
sisting, ground of appeal. It is not
merely that a great satisfaction was
offered to God's justice in the past, but
that the Lord, who offered that satisfaction, now lives in the heavens, at His
Father's right hand, and intercedes for
us with all the influence which His
suffering for us confers upon Him. As
the personal action of God involves His
personal judgment upon our evil, so,
on the other hand, does His personal
character involve His listening to the
perpetual supplications of the Saviour,
pleading for mercy, for long-suffering,
for a further time of grace, for further
aids of God's Spirit, to the souls with
whose weaknesses He sympathizes, with
whose temptations He is acquainted.
The virtue of the Atonement thus consists, not merely in the greatness of the
sacrifice once offered, but in its continual

and living application, by the Saviour's own intercession, before His Father's throne. 'He is able to save them to the uttermost that come unto God by Him, seeing He ever liveth to make intercession for them.' The virtue of His sacrifice is potent in proportion to the personal character of the God and Father to whom it is offered, and before whom it is constantly presented by Him, as our High Priest. There is nothing past, and nothing formal, in the operation of that sacrifice. It is a living Saviour, Whose sufferings are still remembered by Himself and by His Father, Who pleads for us as our Advocate, because He is the propitiation for our sins.

Our personal obligation in return.   Let me add that this personal aspect of the action of the Atonement enforces upon us, in the most solemn way, the fact of our abiding personal obligation to the Saviour. As God's eye ever sees us and judges us, and as the Saviour is ever pleading for us, so should we be ever looking up to Him in humble gratitude and obedience, thankful for the grace which gives us the opportunity and the power to grow into harmony with His will. For the sake of keeping alive in us this perpetual remembrance of His suffering and of His abiding intercession, has He appointed the holy mysteries of the Sacrament of His Body and Blood. Not for the purpose of any propitiatory sacrifice to His Father—for that would be a usurpation of His own office—but 'to the end that we should alway remember the exceeding great love of our Master, and only Saviour, Jesus Christ, thus dying for us, and the innumerable benefits which by His precious blood-shedding He has obtained to us, He hath instituted and ordained holy mysteries, as pledges of His love, and for a continual remembrance of His death, to our great and endless comfort. To Him, therefore, with the Father and the Holy Ghost, let us give (as we are most bounden) continual thanks, submitting ourselves wholly to His holy will and pleasure, and studying to serve Him in true holiness and righteousness all the days of our life.'

THE TESTIMONY TO THE SACRIFICE

2 Cor. xiii. 14.—'The grace of the Lord Jesus Christ, and the love of God, and the communion of the Holy Ghost, be with you all.'

Recapitulation.

AN endeavour has been made, in the three previous discourses, to exhibit some of the chief elements in the atoning work of our Lord, as exhibited to us in His own words and deeds. We have tried to contemplate that work in its actual and living reality, as it presents itself to us in the story of the Gospels, antecedent to the various explanations of its character which have been offered in subsequent theology. The main point which thus becomes prominent is the personal and living action on which it depends, and in which its virtue still

54

subsists. We have to beware of allowing our view of the matter to be determined by such images as that of the payment of a ransom, as though some formal and material transaction had been completed. These are images and analogies, appropriate or permissible enough for certain purposes, but not adequate to express the living reality. Our Lord's work depends, in the first instance, on His personal and direct action, as the Son of God, in declaring His Father's will, and enforcing the claims of spiritual and moral truth upon the Jews of His day. In the next place, when they reject Him, it consists in His deliberately abstaining, out of love for them and for mankind, from enforcing His own and His Father's authority by the power which was at His command, but suffering the consequences Himself, and so bearing, in His own Person, the penalty necessarily involved in the violation of the Divine law, and consequently appealing to men's gratitude and trust by this self-sacrificing love. Being God as well as man, He revealed

to us the love of God,—of God Himself
preferring to suffer, in the human nature
His Son had assumed, rather than assert
His justice against rebellious children.
Finally, as the risen Lord, He acts
personally as our Advocate with the
Father. His past work and past suffering are permanent elements in His personal nature, and He perpetually pleads
for us in the presence of God, interposing the virtue of His sacrifice, and the
claims of His love, between ourselves
and the judgments we incur. The
Atoning work of the Saviour is thus one
continuous course of living action, in
which He, His Father, and ourselves,
are incessantly concerned, and in which
the various personal influences of love,
and righteousness, and self-sacrifice, and
sin, and faith, are perpetually acting and
reacting on one another.

The personal testimony of the Apostles. Now it will assist us in realizing this
living and personal aspect of the work
of the Saviour, if we bear in mind one
circumstance in the relation of the
Apostles to it, which adds a most impressive effect to all the language of the

Epistles on the subject. I refer to the immediate personal relation in which the Apostles stood to our Lord. In all discussions of this subject in subsequent generations there has been a tendency to regard our Lord's sacrifice in the nature of a past event, bearing the usual character of a historical transaction; and doctrinal discussions respecting it have consequently assumed a comparatively abstract form. But an intense vividness is given to all the language of the Epistles respecting it, if we bear in mind that the Apostles are not speaking, like subsequent Christian theologians, of events which occurred beyond the sphere of their experience, and on which they are looking back with comparatively speculative eyes, but that they were speaking and writing of events in which they actually took part, and of a Person whom they knew as intimately as they knew one another. This is pre-eminently the case, for instance, with St Peter and St John, who were admitted to our Lord's closest intimacy, in the most momentous occur-

rences of His life and His passion.
When St John says that 'the blood of
Jesus Christ His Son cleanseth us from
all sin,' he is not merely speaking, like a
subsequent theologian, of the mysterious
efficacy of a past transaction; he is
speaking of the blood which he had
himself seen shed—shed, as it were, in
battle by his side, and in a cause of
which he fully understood the nature.
He had stood by the cross while the
Saviour shed that blood, rather than
avenge Himself of His adversaries, and
had heard the Saviour's words, the evening before, telling him that His blood
was 'shed for many for the remission of
sins.' So when St Peter says that 'ye
were not redeemed with corruptible
things, as silver and gold, from your
vain conversation received by tradition
from your fathers, but with the precious
blood of Christ, as of a lamb without
blemish and without spot,' the words are
instinct, not so much with the doctrinal
accuracy of a theologian, as with the personal remembrance of that spotless Lamb,
Whom St Peter had seen brought to the

slaughter, and opening not His mouth; and towards Whom, alas! he had himself displayed such unfaithfulness. There will appear something infinitely touching, and true to the deepest feelings of human nature, in the prominence which is occupied in the language of the Apostles by the cross and the blood-shedding of the Saviour, when we thus bear in mind their personal participation in those solemn scenes. How could it be otherwise than that that awful scene of the crucifixion, the spectacle of their dear Master, with Whom they had lived in such intimacy and trust, shedding His blood in agony on the cross, had stamped itself with the utmost intensity upon their minds and hearts—that they should thenceforth have, as it were, perpetually present with them the vision of that blood-shedding and that patient suffering, not obscured even by the thought of the glory which had followed! They had lived through that tragedy, and all that led up to it. They had seen their Master's truth and patience; they had witnessed with what agonizing resolve

He had surrendered Himself to the hands of His enemies, and they had seen and felt the very life of His soul, as well as of His body, poured forth in those sufferings of the cross. How could it be otherwise than that that actual vision of the dying and bleeding Saviour — dying and shedding His blood in the face of the world, in love and mercy—should ever be an overpowering element in their thoughts!

The effects of our Lord's sacrifice as seen in the Epistles. This consideration, it may be well to observe, accounts for a circumstance which has sometimes occasioned perplexity on this subject, and even been made a ground of objection to Christian doctrine — the fact, namely, that the subject of our Lord's atonement is less prominent in His own teaching in the Gospels than in the subsequent teaching of His Apostles. Does not the theology of the Epistles, it has been asked, and still more of the Christian Church, give a disproportionate importance to this doctrine, as compared with that which it occupies in our Lord's discourses? The difference in question has, indeed,

been much exaggerated, for our Lord's
references to His coming death, though
reserved and gradually increased, are
yet of the deepest and most impressive
significance. A certain difference, however, in the proportionate place which
the subject holds in the Gospels and
Epistles is apparent; but so far from
being either surprising, or betraying any
lack of harmony in the New Testament,
it is at once a most natural and affecting
token of genuine experience, and an inevitable result of the course of the history.
In the first place, it was obviously impracticable for our Lord to speak fully
and openly of His death beforehand, of
its cause and its consequences, and of
the circumstances by which it would be
attended, without rendering the whole
situation unreal, and preventing the
natural development of the struggle
between God and man, between good
and evil, which He had come to bring
to a final issue. The Jews would not
have been put to the actual trial to
which they were to be submitted; the
Apostles would not have been put to

their own trial ; and consequently the full effect and significance of the Saviour's work would not have been manifested, had not the conflict between righteousness and sin been left to work itself out naturally, without being disturbed by a Divine revelation of its nature and its issue. There are, moreover, various indications in the Gospels how difficult, if not impracticable, it would have been, except by a miraculous supersession of the independent personality of the Apostles, to make them believe beforehand the event which was really to occur. 'They understood none of these things: and this saying was hid from them, neither knew they the things which were spoken' (Luke xviii. 34). After all it is not surprising that they 'could not tell what He said,' for it was beyond human belief that He should meet with such a fate, at the hands of the people among whom they saw and heard Him going about doing good.

The effect could not have been appreciated beforehand. But, even supposing them to have realized it better, how would it have

been possible for a dim foresight of such
an event to produce the same effect as
the actual event itself?   It was not in
human nature to know what so awful
and solemn a scene as the Lord's death
meant, until it had actually been witnessed.   Nothing but the fact itself
could bring the reality home to the
minds of the disciples.   But when it had
actually occurred, when an Apostle
had stood by the cross and seen the
Saviour's death, and had heard His
dying words, then the meaning of His
solemn intimations of it burst upon
their hearts and minds, and it stood out
before their thoughts as the great con-
summation of His life and work.   Thus
the variation between the Gospels and
Epistles in this respect exactly reflects
a real experience, and the course of a
real history, and is one of the most
impressive of unconscious marks of
veracity.   After all, it seems very
strange that it should ever have been
made a complaint against theological
teaching, whether of the Apostles or
of the Church, that it goes beyond

the Gospels. How could it fail to do so? Is it conceivable that such momentous events as the Passion and Death and Resurrection of our Lord could have occurred, without leaving a deep, and a new, mark on the Apostles' thoughts and lives, and without altering, in some degree, the proportion in which truths, old and new alike, appeared to them? It is by great actions that, in the last resort, life and history are moulded; and even our Lord's words, Divine and life-giving as they are, were overshadowed by the supreme effect of His final actions — His Passion, His Death, and His Resurrection.

St Paul's testimony.

The case is similar, if not practically the same, with St Paul, as with the other Apostles. He, too, is not to be considered as writing of events out of his own horizon, or beyond the range of his experience, like subsequent theologians, when speaking of our Lord's death and its consequences. It is striking to realize, when we are reading St Paul's lofty language respecting our Lord, that, in the strictest sense of the word, he was our Lord's contemporary. St Paul was put to death some seventy years after our Lord's birth, so that the earlier half of his life must have been coincident with that of the Saviour; and it adds immense force to all his teaching respecting our Lord's Divine nature and Divine offices, when we reflect that he is not looking back upon Him, as we do, through an atmosphere of centuries of veneration; but that he is deliberately ascribing those supreme powers and offices to a Man of his own generation, who had suffered death at the instance of men then living— men with whom St Paul had been in close and confidential association. There was no possibility of illusion as to the character of the Person respecting whom St Paul was speaking. There could be no myth, and no dream in the matter. It is true St Paul did not share, like St Peter and St John, the intense experiences of our Lord's Passion. Yet the Saviour had personally appeared to him, and had thus given him that sense of personal

E

relation with Himself which infuses such vividness into the language of the other Apostles. When he says, ' God forbid that I should glory, save in the cross of our Lord Jesus Christ, by Whom the world is crucified unto me, and I unto the world,' he is speaking of a cross erected in his own day, and of the death upon it of One Who had visibly appeared to himself, and Whom he had himself once persecuted. There is surely a special and unique reality attached to the teaching of the Apostles, respecting the atoning work of our Lord, when viewed in this light. We, it is to be feared, too often look back upon it as a mysterious transaction, out of the range of living human experience—the subject of religious thought, and a matter, alas ! of theological controversy. But the cross of Christ, the death of Christ, the blood of Christ—these were all sacred, but actual, realities within the experience of the Apostles, and they are speaking of what they had ' seen, and heard, and handled,' with only too terrible a naturalness.

But do not these considerations throw a correspondingly vivid light upon their language respecting the atoning efficacy of our Lord's work? What the Apostles say about it is not to them merely doctrine or theory, but fact. In subsequent generations, for example, there has been much discussion among theologians respecting vicarious sacrifice, and its legitimate place in a scheme of redemption. But to an Apostle like St Peter, there was no possibility of such a question arising. He had seen our Lord suffer, in love and patience, for offences not His own, the Just for the unjust. He knew, from personal experience, the innocence of that Lamb without blemish and without spot; and he had lived, in bitter remorse and shame, through that night and day, when our Lord consented to be delivered into the hands of wicked men, and to suffer death upon the cross. What a mockery it would have seemed to him to be discussing, in cold blood, in what sense a sacrifice could be offered by Christ, and how it could be efficacious for the forgiveness of others? As a matter of bitter fact, he had seen it offered by Christ, not for Himself, but for others. St John, too, had attended every stage of the cruel history; he had been with his Master the evening before, and had heard Him deliberately saying that He was about to shed His blood for many, for the remission of sins; he had seen that death perfected, and had heard the prayer, 'Father, forgive them, for they know not what they do'; and could he doubt that that prayer had been answered, for all for whom it was offered? When St Peter tells us that even the angels desire to look into the mysteries of the Saviour's work, we may venture to feel assured that he knew it was not for men fully to understand it. But that Christ died for others, that He prayed for others, and that that death and those prayers must have been efficacious for others —of these things, as he believed in a just and good God, and trusted his Master's dying words, he could have no more doubt than of his own existence.

St John had witnessed the loving and
holy soul of the Saviour struggling
against men's evil, denouncing it, ex-
horting them against it, pleading with
them to renounce it; and then submitting to be killed by them, as a last
appeal to their hearts and to His
Father's mercy, and, in the midst of
His agonies, praying to His Father to
have compassion on them—and how
can he fail to have been impressed, as
with the greatest moral reality in the
world, with the fact that the suffering
Saviour was a propitiation for our sins,
and had established at once an eternal
claim upon the mercy of God, and an
equal claim upon the allegiance and
obedience of himself and his fellow-
men? The explanation, by scientific
theology, of the relative operation of
the Divine attributes, and of the development of the Divine scheme of
creation and redemption, may well be
worthy of endless meditation; and
eternity may be, and must be, occupied
in apprehending its wonders. But the
essential fact is as present, and as over-

powering, to the vision of Apostles like Peter, John, and Paul, as some great convulsion of nature to the eyes of those on whom it suddenly bursts in all its grandeur and awefulness. Christ dying in love and mercy, sacrificing His life for men, pleading with God for them — this is not a matter of theological theory, but of vivid personal fact.

In short, our Lord's life, passion, death, and resurrection, together with the assurances He gave His Apostles of His perpetual presence with them, and of His future return, established them, and establish all who accept their testimony, in a living and personal relation with the Saviour, and with His Spirit, of the deepest and most affecting character. That life, death, and resurrection revealed in the Divine nature the most intense personal life, in living participation with the moral struggles of men and women; and the words of the text bore to the Apostles, and should bear to us, this living meaning and personal message. 'The grace of the Lord Jesus Christ, and the love of God, and

'The grace of our Lord JesusChrist.'

the communion of the Holy Ghost' were
to them, and should be to us, the expression of the personal and present
action of those Divine Persons. 'Ye
know,' says St Paul, 'the grace of our
Lord Jesus Christ, how that, though
He was rich, yet for your sakes He
became poor, that ye, through His
poverty, might be rich.' The Grace
of the Lord Jesus Christ is not only,
nor in the first instance, that special
aid which He bestows by His spiritual
influences ; it is, first, and above
all, the grace, the personal grace,
which condescended to our weakness,
which suffered the consequences of our
sins, which submitted to our violence
and injustice, which endured to shed
His blood in patience and agony. The
Love of God is not only His general
benevolence to all His children, but
that love which endured that His only-
begotten Son, in Whom He was well
pleased, should endure all this bitterness
and misery, instead of being delivered
from it by the just execution of the
Divine vengeance upon His enemies

and persecutors; and the Communion of the Holy Ghost is the fellowship of our spirits with the Spirit of this gracious Lord, and of His loving and patient Father, the privilege of being admitted to their society in a similar sense to that in which the Apostles were admitted to it, and of thus living in the perpetual comfort of such love and grace as the Saviour showed in His passion.

'In remembrance of me.'

The reality and depth of our Christian life depend, in the first instance, upon our living in the sense of this fellowship, and realizing the Saviour's work for us with a similar personal vividness to that with which, as we have seen, it was present to the minds of the Apostles. It is this which constitutes the preciousness of the Sacrament of the Holy Communion, considered as a remembrance of the death of Christ. It is, indeed, an important truth that that holy Sacrament is not only a memorial of the Lord's death and passion—not, as is sometimes said, 'a bare memorial.' It is also the communion, to those who receive it aright, of the body and blood of Christ. But let not this precious and mysterious spiritual grace obscure to us how much is involved in the fact that such a memorial it is. Its importance in this respect would seem especially emphasized by the Saviour's words, 'Do this in remembrance of Me.' It is, in fact, in proportion as we remember Him in the sense we are now considering, in proportion as we realize His personal action and suffering on our behalf, in proportion as His death, and the shedding of His blood for our sakes, as for the sakes of all mankind, is present as a living reality to the eye of faith, that we are fitted to receive the further benefits of that Holy Sacrament. But let us thus remember Him, remember Him in His grace and love, in His intense desire for our righteousness and our deliverance from all evil, and in the bitter sacrifice He made for that end, and we shall then live, more and more, in 'the grace of the Lord Jesus Christ, and the love of God, and the communion of the Holy Spirit.'

V

THE SUFFICIENCY OF THE SACRIFICE

HEB. ix. 13, 14.—'For if the blood of bulls and of goats, and the ashes of an heifer sprinkling the unclean, sanctifieth to the purifying of the flesh : how much more shall the blood of Christ, Who through the Eternal Spirit offered Himself without spot to God, purge your conscience from dead works, to serve the living God?'

The Jewish sacrifices. THESE verses bring before us, with singular comprehensiveness and vividness, the parallel which is presented by the sacred writer between the Jewish sacrifices and the sacrifice offered by our Lord, alike in their nature and in their effect. It is a parallel which must have carried a force to the Hebrews, whom he addressed, beyond what we can easily realize. But if we would appreciate it, we must endeavour to recall the impressive, and even painful, prominence which was held in the ritual of the old Covenant by that element of it on which the Apostle is here chiefly dwelling—the shedding of blood. This was not an occasional element of the ancient ritual, but its central, its most conspicuous, and its constant, characteristic. The circumstances of our Saviour's purification of the Temple are sufficient to remind us of the extent to which animals were sacrificed on the great festivals. 'The Jews' Passover,' we read, 'was at hand, and Jesus went up to Jerusalem, and found in the Temple those that sold oxen and sheep and doves, and the changers of money sitting.' The Court of the Gentiles had been transformed into a market for the sale of these animals. We are told in the Talmud of thousands of sheep being thus introduced into the Temple Courts. The number, that were sometimes slaughtered, may be imagined from the fact that Herod alone is said to have sacrificed three hundred oxen at the consecration of the new Temple; and Josephus adds that 'Herod's example was followed by each, according to his ability, so that it was impossible to state the number correctly.' Nor was it only on great occasions that this slaughter of animals marked the ritual of the law; but day by day the regular sacrifices, and the purifications by which the important events of Jewish family life were attended, required a similar immolation of victims. The presentation, for instance, of the first-born child to the Lord, as in the case of the Virgin Mary, required that she should 'offer a sacrifice, according to that which is said in the law of the Lord, a pair of turtledoves, or two young pigeons.' In a word, as the Apostle summarily says in this chapter, 'almost all things are by the law purged with blood, and without shedding of blood is no remission.' It must be obvious what an immense impression such a continual and lavish outpouring of blood must have tended to

produce upon the minds of the Jews.
They could not conceive of an ap-
proach to God which was not prepared by some offering of blood, by
the sacrifice of some life. Their whole
mind was impregnated with the sight
of bloodshed in sacrificial worship ;
and the sacrifice of life, impressed
upon their minds with this painful
vividness, was the very centre of their
religious worship.

Now it is with this deep feeling and The neces-
conviction that the sacred writer has shedding.
to deal, in endeavouring to reassure the
Hebrews with respect to the adequacy
of the new Covenant to which they
had been introduced, and in which he
desired to confirm them ; and he therefore has to show that a sacrifice had
been offered which was sufficient to
supply the place of this vast system
of animal sacrifices. According to
the law, under which they had lived,
and which was to them the first
principle of existence, they were de-
pendent on the continual shedding of
the blood of bulls and of goats to

make atonement for their sins, and to
qualify them for the service of God.
If they contracted any ceremonial de-
filement, especially by that contact with
death which was unavoidable in the
circumstances of daily life, they required to be sprinkled with water, in
which the ashes of a burnt heifer had
been mixed, before they could re-enter
the congregation of God's people
Artificial as, in some respects, these
various ceremonial defilements seemed,
they none the less corresponded with
a deep natural sense of unworthiness
in the presence of a God of perfect
holiness; and they had succeeded in
stamping upon the minds of the Jews,
with extraordinary depth, the necessity
for the most absolute and scrupulous
purity and righteousness in approach-
ing Him. It will be seen, in the light
of these considerations, what an immense weight the sacred writer's argument must needs attach to the sacrifice
and bloodshedding of Christ. He is
proclaiming, not to Gentiles but to
Hebrews, that one sacrifice has been

made, one offering of blood, which is
sufficient to purify for ever those for
whom it was offered, and which is
capable of standing, to all eternity, in
the place of those innumerable and
never-ceasing sacrifices of the Jewish
law. If the Gospel were to be accept-
able to the Hebrews, it must satisfy
this requirement. The whole Hebrew
Ritual would have been a mockery,
and almost a barbarous one, unless
some tremendous expiation for sin was
foreshadowed by it, and unless some
sacred blood were some day to be shed,
which would take the place of that fearful ritual.

The author accordingly is concerned
to enforce, in the deepest and most
touching manner, the profound and
perfect character of the sacrifice offered
by our Lord. For this purpose he
depicts in few, but intensely affecting, words the supreme holiness and
graciousness, the Divine perfection of
our Saviour's nature. He was the
brightness of His Father's glory, and
the express image of His Person ; and,

The perfec-
tion of our
Lord's sacri-
fice.

taking on Himself flesh and blood, He
submitted to all the trials and sufferings
which were requisite to develop the
entire perfection of His human nature.
' He learned obedience by the things
which He suffered, and being made
perfect, He became the author of
eternal salvation to all them that obey
Him.' As man, as well as God, He
became a High Priest, ' holy, harmless,
undefiled, separate from sinners, and
made higher than the heavens'; and
in this character, possessing this absolute
priestly purity, He made an offering of
His own perfect flesh and blood, His
human nature, in all its comprehension,
from its highest faculties to its mortal
frame, to bear the consequences of
human evil, and to be, for the whole
human race, all and more than all, that
the Jewish sacrifices had been for those
for whom they were instituted. The
perfect nature of this sacrifice is ex-
pressed with comprehensive intensity in
the words of the text. ' Through the
Eternal Spirit,' He offered ' Himself
without spot to God.' He was ab-

solutely without spot. Neither in
body nor in soul was there the
slightest blemish upon His perfect
nature. Viewing Him in this character, there was something inexpres-
sibly terrible in the fact, that that
soul should be sacrificed, and that
body cruelly put to death, in consequence of the evil and the malice of
corrupt and wicked men. Using the
word 'sacrifice' in its commonest and
most ordinary sense, there never was
such a sacrifice made, or dreamed of,
as when our Lord, in all the perfection
of His nature, was cast out from among
mankind, and abandoned by a cowardly
Governor to the hatred of the people
whom that Governor feared to offend.
Before we consider the cause, it is
sufficiently impressive, and even appal-
ling, to reflect that the most precious
life, the most precious incarnation and
manifestation of all that is most exalted
in the world, should thus have been
sacrificed to human wickedness and
hate. This, accordingly, is the first
point on which the Apostle insists.

F

That blood, so shed, was infinitely more precious than the torrents of animal blood with which the temple courts had flowed for centuries.

The spirit by which it was offered.

But pass, from the value of that which was offered, to the spirit and the manner in which the offering was made. Christ, 'through the Eternal Spirit, offered Himself without spot to God.' That is to say, it was by the deliberate action of His eternal spiritual nature, by His Divine, as well as human, will, that He made Himself that offering. The Spirit of Christ, subsisting from all eternity, and throughout all eternity, was, as it were, the altar on which that sacrifice of His body and blood, and of the soul which they enshrined, was made. It was not a passing offering, like the comparatively brief, or even sudden, sacrifices which are made for great causes by ordinary men and women. But by virtue of an eternal will and purpose, our Saviour laid down His life, and shed His blood upon the cross, in order to offer an adequate atonement for the sins of His fellow-men, and thus to abolish—if they will only place themselves under His shelter, by accepting Him as their Saviour and their King—the necessity for that terrible expiation on their own part, which the Jewish sacrifices had symbolized. These are the two points on which the writer insists, in order to assure his Hebrew kinsmen of the adequacy of the sacrifice he proclaimed to take the place of their whole sacrificial system. An Eternal Spirit, looking back in its determinations to all the past, and forward in its powers and its resolves to the infinite future, stands, as it were, in the centre of all space and time, sacrificing a perfect nature, shedding an infinitely precious blood, to make an Atonement, on the part of mankind, to the God Whose holiness they had outraged. Is not the substitution, the Apostle exclaims, more than sufficient? 'If the blood of bulls and of goats, and the ashes of an heifer sprinkling the unclean sanctifieth to the purifying of the flesh, how much more shall the blood of Christ, Who through the Eternal Spirit offered Himself without spot to God, purge your conscience from dead works to serve the living God?' 'How much more!' To us it may, at first, seem almost an unworthy comparison. But when we remember what has been recalled of the lavish sacrifices which the Jewish law required, and the immense efforts of expiation which they symbolized, we appreciate in some degree the momentous influence which the sacred writer attributes to the Saviour's death, to the shedding of His blood, and the offering of His body.

'Without shedding of blood is no remission.'

Such appears the nature of the writer's argument in relation to the Jews, and it still retains enormous force, even in its technical application, as illustrating to us the value of the sacrifice offered by our Saviour's death. But if we would fully apply the argument to ourselves, we must endeavour to realize the fact that the whole Jewish Ritual we have been considering, though arbitrary and positive in its particular prescriptions, did but serve to bring into prominence what is the central and most terrible reality of life. The rule, that without shedding of blood is no remission, is not merely a Jewish ceremonial prescription, but may be regarded as a statement of the chief condition of human progress and life. In quiet times, we easily fall into the habit of dwelling solely on the peaceful progress of human affairs, and of looking upon bloodshed, as for instance in war, as an unnatural and horrible exception. Yet, if we look at history, we shall find, as a plain matter of fact, that civilization, and the Church itself, has been built up at the cost of continual bloodshed. The animals slaughtered under the Jewish law were, after all, but a faint representation of the millions of human victims who have been sacrificed, in generation after generation, since the career of the human race began, in the assertion of the various causes, principles, claims, by which men have struggled upward to their present condition. War itself may be regarded, from this point of view, as a sort of sacrificial system, established in the very nature of things, as necessary for the conduct and progress of human affairs, in our present condition. It is of no avail pleasing ourselves with theories of an ideal condition of human life, and forgetting the reality. As a matter of fact, the world is so constituted that it has not been able to advance, or even to exist, without the perpetual shedding of blood. We know that it is going on in various quarters of the earth at the present moment. If we are gradually bringing under control and order uncivilized tribes in Asia and Africa, we have of late been too sadly reminded of the sacrifice of life, of the shedding of blood, by which those advances are being won, and by which, we know too well, they will have to be won in the future. It would seem as though, whether men like to shut their eyes to it or not, the law proclaimed in the Scriptures asserts itself irresistibly; death and bloodshed are dogging the steps of human sin, and the sad penalty is being inexorably exacted. Such facts and realities are a strange commentary on those philosophical theories which would make the promotion of religion and morality a mere philanthropic enterprise, to be accomplished by kind feelings and genial intentions. Great causes mean great sacrifices; and the highest cause of all, that of truth and righteousness, means the greatest sacrifice of all—the sacrifice of blood, and of the best blood.

In view, in short, of these facts, it is more than strange, it seems like child's play, that men should sometimes, and too often, be found seriously arguing whether human sin demands an expiation, and involves such penalties as the Scriptures speak of. The Scriptures only interpret the penalties; the infliction of them is a mere matter of fact, of constant experience. The expiation is being continually exacted by the very constitution of nature. If, as St Paul says, we are all members of one body, so that the human race may be contemplated as having one life, then may we,

The sacrificial expiation of sin a fact of life.

and must we, contemplate the whole
body of mankind as one bleeding
victim, suffering, on the altar of history and of the earth, for its sins and
errors. But if this be so, if, in the Divine
constitution of things, it be an unalter-
able fact that suffering and death must
atone for sin, what an infinite blessing
to be assured that the Head of the
human race, the perfect Son of man
and Son of God, has Himself taken
the chief share of this suffering, and
has sanctified it by the infinite value of
His precious blood. What a grace it
casts upon the long sufferings of mankind to know that, in so far as they
have been faithfully and truly borne,
they are associated with the sacrifice of
Him, Who, through the Eternal Spirit,
offered Himself without spot to God.
And as, with reference to the Jewish
sacrifices, the sacred writer points to
the blood of Christ as rendering them
unnecessary, and for ever abolishing
them, so may we be assured that that
Divine Sacrifice of Christ will gradually,
but certainly, abolish in the end—

though, it may be, only in the end of the world—all those sacrifices of his fellow-sufferers, which have been endured since the world began, and that the bloodshed and misery of the human race will then be for ever removed.—

But let us, in conclusion, take to heart the application to our own life of this inspired appeal. 'How much more,' he says, 'shall the blood of Christ purge your conscience from dead works to serve the living God?' In other words, he seems to say, could we but 'remember the exceeding great love of our Master, and only Saviour, Jesus Christ, thus dying for us,' could we bear always in mind the precious blood He shed, the fact that His very life blood is eternally sprinkled, as it were, upon all things that are true, just and pure, then, but not till then, should we possess an adequate motive, and an adequate power, for resisting those evil desires, those corrupt affections, that lack of patience and humility, which are our weakness and our shame, and then would our conscience be purged and stimulated to

'The blood of Jesus Christ, His Son, cleanseth us from all sin.

good works. What a transcendent force
is introduced into the moral and spiritual
world when, in all our struggles to be
just, pure and true, we are associated—
nay when we are united—with the death
and passion of our Saviour Christ. Even
if, for a moment, we regarded the matter
from a merely human point of view,
that death and passion have for ever
hallowed the struggle after truth and
goodness by the shedding of the most
precious blood the world has ever
known. Most of us, at one time or
another, have had occasion to realize
how the shedding of blood, the voluntary endurance of torture and agony,
stirs the soul to its depths, cements a
society and hallows a cause. Surely if
men thought, judging merely as men,
that in every untrue, unjust, impure or
impatient, word or deed, they were
doing despite to Jesus Christ, and
spurning the blood He shed in vindication of truth and goodness, they might
shrink from sin as involving them in all
the shame and ingratitude of treachery.
This influence might surely be felt if

Jesus Christ were a man like ourselves, Whose life was past centuries ago, and Whose memory alone was sacred. But regard Him as the sacred writer here describes Him, as eternally offering Himself, through the Eternal Spirit, to God the Father, in propitiation for our sins ; regard Him as the Christian does, as now living and present with each one of us; believe that, at each moment, the righteous voice you hear within you, pleading with you to be patient, humble, obedient, true, or pure, is that of the Lord Jesus, Who suffered and died upon the cross in patient obedience to that same duty—and is there a heart that could resist his appeal ? To the Apostles, and their immediate followers, this thought was always present. The blood of Christ cleansed them from all sin. It was not only an atonement for the past, a propitiatory offering to God ; it was ever present to their thoughts, purging their consciences from dead works to serve the living God. It was sprinkled, as it were, upon the entrance to their souls, forbidding the destroying enemy of sin to enter; and whatever their exhortation, it was clenched with the appeal : 'Forasmuch as ye know that ye were not redeemed with corruptible things, but with the precious blood of Christ.'

The Christian privilege.

In short, it is the privilege of Christians —a privilege to be exercised in fear and trembling, but not to be foregone—to sanctify every duty, however humble, to intensify every dictate of the conscience, however slight, to strengthen every spiritual aspiration and resolve, by viewing it as united with the Passion and the Death of Christ. The appeal of the text thus imparts into our moral and spiritual life, into every act and every thought of that life, the most intense and vivid of all natural influences, immeasurably heightened by the Divine character and nature of the person by whom it is exercised. There are, indeed, innumerable influences ever around us, thank God, to recall us from evil, and to inspire us to good works. Let us cherish them, and be thankful for them all. But if we would realize our highest motives and our fullest powers, let us never forget this supreme appeal: 'How much more shall the blood of Christ, Who through the Eternal Spirit offered Himself without spot to God, purge your conscience from dead works, to serve the living God?'

THE END

Colston and Coy. Limited, Printers, Edinburgh